Corinne Maier

Bonjour Laziness

Corinne Maier works part-time as an economist for EDF, a French corporation. She is also a practicing psychoanalyst and the author of nine books. She lives in France.

Bonjour Laziness

Why Hard Work Doesn't Pay

Corinne Maier

Translated from the French by Sophie Hawkes

Vintage Books
A Division of Random House, Inc.
New York

FIRST VINTAGE BOOKS EDITION, SEPTEMBER 2006

The Library of Congress has cataloged the Pantheon edition as follows:
Maier, Corinne.
[Bonjour Paresse. English]
Bonjour Laziness : jumping off the corporate ladder / translated from the French by Sophie Hawkes.
p. cm.
Includes bibliographical references.
1. Corporate culture. 2. Work ethic. 3. Laziness. I. Title.
HM791.M3413 2005
650.1—dc22 2005045827

Vintage ISBN-10: 1-4000-9628-6
Vintage ISBN-13: 978-1-4000-9628-2

Author photograph © Eric Robert
Book design by Iris Weinstein

www.vintagebooks.com

Printed in the United States of America
10 9 8 7 6 5 4 3 2 1

Contents

Bonjour Laziness

Introduction

Business Is Not Humanistic

"Never work," wrote the philosopher Guy Debord. It's a great idea but hard to put into practice. Besides, lots of people are going to go to work in business—and business, especially big business, has always generously provided jobs. Oddly enough, the corporate world is shrouded in mystery. Is the subject taboo? Let's talk about it without pretense or corporate-speak.

Hear ye, hear ye, middle managers of the corporate world! This provocative book is aimed at "demoralizing" you—that is, in the sense of making you lose your morale. It will help you take advantage of the firm you work for, which up until now has been taking advantage of you. It will explain why it's in your best interest to work as little as possible, and how to undermine the system from within, without appearing to do so.

Is *Bonjour Laziness* cynical? Yes—intentionally so—but business is hardly humanistic! It does not want the best for you and does not practice what it preaches, as we can see from all the financial scandals in the headlines and the social plans that fall by the wayside. It's not much fun, except when we seize the chance to make fun of it, as we are doing here.

Can Disenchantment Solve the Problem of Business?

Millions of people work in business, but its world is opaque. This is because the people who talk about it the most—and I mean university professors—have never worked there; they aren't *in the know.* The people in the know keep quiet; consultants who are in a hurry to start their own companies keep their lips sealed, since it's against their best interests to saw off the branches they're sitting on. The same goes for the management gurus who bombard the business world with advice, starting ridiculous fads they don't even believe in. This explains why all the indigestible books on "management" are to the business world what manuals of constitutional law are to politics: hardly a way to understand the tricks of the trade.*

Still, people are beginning to talk about the corporate world as it really is. Fiction has paved the way, no longer hesitating to take as a backdrop the hushed corridors of Arthur Andersen (the accounting firm for Enron, which went bankrupt in 2002). This is a good idea, difficult as it is to imagine Romeo and Juliet discussing cash flow or management, creating mergers, organizing joint ventures, calculating synergies, or drafting org charts. The corporate world, alas, has no use for noble passions such as courage, generosity, or devotion to the public good. It doesn't make us dream. And yet . . . if it's not the primary arena where people

*I'm a little hard on them and must admit I'm a bit jealous. While my cushy job in business is better paid than theirs, it's less chic. Okay, I won't deny it: some academics, sociologists in particular, have produced interesting works on business.

energetically accomplish real things, why do people with degrees from higher institutions traditionally and overwhelmingly choose to exercise their talents in business—preferably big business?

When I first started working, big business had wind in its sails, and everything was happening as though business grew out of the same movement toward social mobility and spirit of freedom of the 1960s. However, I quickly became disenchanted. And I've been disenchanted for a long time now and have had the time to notice that they lied to us. Not only is the corporate world boring, it's potentially brutal. Its true face has been all the more visible since the Internet bubble burst and financial scandals have been gracing the front pages. The collapse of the stock prices of Vivendi, Enron, Lucent, Global Crossing, and the like has rubbed salt in everyone's wounds by blitzing the pension funds of thousands of shareholders, until now blissfully confident in these firms' big-talking CEOs. Worst of all were the disasters of 2003, which revealed the dark side of business as layoffs multiplied at AT&T, Lucent, DaimlerChrysler, Oracle . . .

It's curtains for business. Just look at the facts: it's no longer a place of success. The chance to advance in society is blocked. The security offered by university degrees has decreased, pension funds are at risk, and careers are no longer guaranteed. The 1960s, when we were excited by progress and assured of job security, are ancient history. The wind has changed and, to escape it, crowds of the educated are already begging for obscure positions as low-level bureaucrats.

The corporate world no longer offers many chances for planning one's future. The generations behind us will have to obtain even more degrees to hold less and less rewarding positions or to engage in less and less attractive activities. I've already told my son and daughter: "Darlings, please promise never, ever, to work in business when you grow up. Daddy and Mommy would be so disappointed!"

The lack of individual and social prospects is such that the children of the middle class, breeding ground for the recruitment of business managers, should decide to bail out. How? By heading for professions less integrated into the capitalist game (the arts, the sciences, teaching) or by withdrawing partially from the corporate world, middle finger elegantly raised as a parting gesture. That's what I'm doing: I work only part-time, devoting my best hours to other, more exciting activities.* Follow my example, ye small-time yuppies and wage slaves, ye wretched of the service sector, grunts of the economic process, brothers and sisters led by the nose by dreary, servile little bosses and forced to dress like puppets all week long and to waste time in useless meetings and bogus seminars.

And in the meantime, since cutting out takes some planning, why not undermine the system from within while you're inside? Passively ape the manager's behavior, imitate his speech and gestures, but without "getting involved." You won't be the first: according to a recent Gallup survey, 17 percent of American professionals are "actively disengaged" from their work, which means that they have adopted so unconstructive an attitude that it verges on sabotage. A mere 29 percent of American middle managers are "crazy about" their jobs and consider themselves "actively engaged" in their work. You must admit that's very

*Such as? Okay, since we're spilling our guts here: psychoanalysis and writing. But there are loads of other fascinating things to do (both paid and unpaid, but that's not the point), such as raising donkeys, cobbling together a terrific home sound system, organizing parties, becoming an activist in the association of your choosing, cultivating a vineyard, trading fossils, painting, flirting on the beach . . .

little. As for the other 54 percent—those who fall into the "not-engaged" category—the firm tries to "motivate" them: seminars to buck up deadbeat managers en masse are on the rise. Obviously, if you're looking for ways to incite wage earners to roll up their sleeves, it means they don't give a damn about their jobs! My grandfather, a self-made wholesaler, never got up in the morning wondering if he was "motivated." He just did his job. It was as simple as that.

Adopting an attitude of "active disengagement" won't do you any harm as long as it's discreet. In any case, you are surrounded by incompetent coworkers and cowards, and they'll never notice your lack of passion. And rest assured that if by chance they do notice it, they won't dare say anything, because to discipline you would adversely affect your boss in two ways: first of all, it would make public the fact that he (or she) was unable to supervise you correctly; secondly, a possible reprimand would limit your possibilities of transfer! It's thanks to this *omertà* that some people get outrageous promotions: their supervisors will do anything to get rid of them—even kick them upstairs. One small step for mankind, one giant step for hypocrisy. . . .

Pierre de Coubertin, the founder of the modern Olympics, said that the important thing is to participate. Today the most important thing is to participate as little as possible. And this may even be enough—who knows?—to reduce the system to dust. (The communists twiddled their thumbs for seventy years and one fine day the Berlin Wall came crashing down.) In the meantime, let's not delude ourselves: there's nothing to be gained in waiting for a revolution, for humanity never ceases repeating the same mistakes, with its red tape, its extremely mediocre leaders, and, in more dangerous times, when people get really worked up, its gallows. These are the principles that will help you to understand the corporate world as it really is, not as it pretends to be.

A New Way of Reading Tea Leaves

In business, when someone says something to you or when you read a document, there are certain keys that must be used to unlock the meaning. This method of decoding, through the use of a reading chart, will help you to read business like an open book because business is a text that speaks, communicates, and writes. It does so rather poorly, true, and so much the better, for this makes the task of decoding and understanding it all the more amusing.

Here's how to decipher the code:

- **Reverse the signs.** The more big business talks about something, the less of it there is. For example, it "values" jobs just at the moment when they disappear; it revels in "autonomy" when in fact you have to fill out forms in triplicate for the slightest trifle and ask the advice of six people to make insignificant decisions; it harps on "ethics" while believing in absolutely nothing.

- **Follow the circular reasoning.** Business talk is circular, like a snake eating its own tail. All you have to do is take an idea and follow it to the end and without fail you come back to the beginning. The corporate world is a place where, very often, the business meeting is the ultimate goal of the work, and action the ultimate goal of action—unless it's the other way around.

- **Detect the idiocy of lies.** Taking stock of a situation is most difficult in business, and with experience you will learn that sometimes the best answer to any question is "Whatever you say, sir." For example, when your bosses tell you, "Our staff is our best asset," or "Your ideas are important to us," this is a meaningless banality, for everyone knows that such a world does not exist. On the other hand, the statement "With us you can do many jobs, have great adventures, and be responsible for varied, innovative assignments and projects" is clearly flimflam. And when a manager claims, "I haven't heard a word about it," or "I practice consensus politics," it's usually a lie. The marriage of stupidity and hypocrisy is fruitful, giving rise to the practice of contemporary business administration, which some have pompously baptized "the New Management."

- **Do a reality check.** Some things that are quite manageable in daily life become difficult in the business world. And when they are merely difficult in day-to-day existence, they're completely impossible in the workplace. For example, any effort at large-scale reorganization—that is, any project spanning more than two years and, more generally, anything that has not already been done—is inevitably doomed to failure.

- **Put things in perspective.** You must put things and events back into context. The firm cannot be separated from the world in which it flourishes—or, as in the current economic environment, in which it declines. It is but a symbol of a world that has foundered in lies, ceaselessly postponing the final deathblow by virtue of enormous bribes and indignant posturing.

Warning: If You Are an Individualist, Walk On By

To the individualist, my brother in arms and kindred spirit: this book is not for you, since business is not for you. Working in big business only shackles the individual, who, left to his own devices and using his own powers of comprehension, might begin to reflect, doubt, or even to question authority! And that's just not acceptable. If the individual finds himself having new ideas, he shouldn't under any circumstances let them disturb the group. It's clear that in a world where one is advised to be flexible, to change tack every five minutes, and to stay in sync with the others, the individualist is a troublemaker, a tinderbox of discord. In addition, corporations prefer the cowardly, the insipid, the obsequious guy who bends over backwards and plays the game, fits the mold, and finally manages to do his thing without making waves.

Not only is our wild individualist incapable of following like the rest, but when he does have strong opinions, he is loath to compromise, which arouses mistrust—and rightly so. Personnel officers can smell him coming: "inflexible," "obstinate," and "stubborn" are adjectives that abound in his personnel file. And it's considered uncool to be inflexible; uncool to leave work when you're done working; uncool to skip the Christmas office party, or not to contribute to the envelope for your colleague's retirement; uncool to go back to your hotel like a whirlwind as soon as the meeting with the partners from Taiwan is over; uncool not to drink coffee offered to you during the coffee break; uncool to pack a brown paper bag when everyone else eats in the cafeteria.

People who act this way are considered the office cacti by their colleagues, for conviviality—in the form of drinks, conventional jokes, chumminess, and hypocritical pecks on the cheek—is mandatory. One must appear to conform in these matters or risk being ostracized. Yet, what if our prickly friends have actually got it right, and understand not to cross the line between work and personal life? Perhaps they have realized that to be always available for a long list of unlikely projects—half of which are completely idiotic, the other half ill-conceived—is a little like changing sexual partners twice a year. When you're twenty, the idea might have a certain charm; but over the years, frankly, it becomes a chore.

The New Management is an erection on command.

Here, in six chapters, are all the reasons you'll ever need to disengage.

1.

Business Speaks an Incomprehensible No-Man's-Language

The most striking thing about the business world is its jargon. It does not have a monopoly on this, since we live in a world of claptrap. Universities, the media, and psychoanalysts are masters of the genre. Still, business jargon is particularly deadly, enough to utterly discourage the workplace hero, the Stakhanovite, lying dormant in you. (Never mind if you don't know the meaning of "Stakhanovite." Read blithely on, for hero workers didn't make the cut in the casting of this book. In fact, they are very rare in the business world. There used to be some in the Soviet Union, but it's anyone's guess what became of them.)

Hello, Gibberish

When I first started working, I didn't understand a word my colleagues were saying, and it took me a moment to realize that this was normal. A superb example of this ridiculous language is found in French novelist Michel Houellebecq's book *Extension du domaine de la lutte* (*Whatever*), a work that influenced a whole generation (my own):

> Before I joined this firm, I was given a voluminous tome entitled *Development Plan for the Ministry of Agriculture's Data-Processing System*. . . . It was intended, according to the introduction, to be an "attempt to predefine various archetypal situations, developed in the context of a targeted objective." . . . I quickly flipped through the book, underlining the

> funniest sentences in pencil. For example, "The strategic level consists of the creation of a system of global information promulgated through the integration of diversified, heterogenous subsystems."

Such is the nature of gibberish. It is the ground zero of language, where the words no longer mean anything at all.

This is because the business world has a dream: that human language, far from being the window or mirror that certain bright intellectuals believe it to be, can be reduced to a mere "tool," a new code that is the essence of pure information, so long as one masters the key. This fantasy of a transparent, rational, simple-to-acquire language translates into a true no-man's-language. Pretending to be dispassionate and unprejudiced, and purged of all imagination, this language envelops all statement in a cloud of scientific detachment. Words no longer serve to convey meaning and actually obscure the links between events by covering up the causes that produce them. This deliberately abstruse and incomprehensible no-man's-language ends up resembling an impenetrable jargon derived from the pseudosciences. Its unintelligibility is perfect for seducing people who feel more informed the more muddled their ideas are. The more technical and abstract the language used in business, the more persuasive businesspeople believe it to be.

Its jargon is a fixed response to the complexity of real life. Certain mechanisms are set in motion, but they proceed in an inexorable, wooden manner, giving the impression that no people are actually involved. Examples: "A watchdog unit has been established," "An information-gathering program has been instituted," "A balance sheet has been drafted." One might think that nothing ever happens in business. This impersonal language, with its emphasis on processes, gives us the illusion of being protected. Nothing can happen here: no surprises, no excitement—unless you count being fired! This is the peace not of the brave, but of the middle manager. History happens to other people, the riffraff who inhabit the margins of the civilized world and kill one another because they haven't got anything better to do.

Only communist regimes have churned out more jargon than modern business. George Orwell was the first to understand that Soviet jargon was not a jargon like any other, laughable and inoffensive, but a genuine metamorphosis of language triggered by ideology. In *1984* he intuited the role played by newspeak in the functioning of the totalitarian state. For business *is* a totalitarian power, in a "lite" kind of way. It doesn't pretend that work sets you free (*Arbeit macht frei* in German), although some dare to make this claim from time to time.

The real problem is that by abolishing style, jargon denies the individual: no memo or note should ever betray its author. Each document is polished in such a way that the ritual jargon peculiar to each firm is respected. A collective way of writing is established. Whatever the subject at hand, the content is squashed flat under a steamroller. No speaker is responsible for it: he or she merely parrots words already spoken and thus business-speak is not addressed to anyone in particular. It's no surprise that it puts you to sleep! It represents a unique example of a language divorced from thought but that hasn't died as a result of this separation (yet).

Business-speak follows five basic rules:

- It makes the simple sound complicated. It says "initialize" instead of "begin," which is far too ordinary; "finalize" instead of the mundane "finish"; "position" for the down-to-earth "place."

- It chooses a vocabulary that makes it sound more important than it really is. "Coordinate" and "optimize" are weightier than "carry out" and "improve." But "resolve" rules the pantheon of verbs, beating out "steer" and "supervise" by a nose. And there's certainly no lack of words ending in "-ance" or "-ence" and "-ency," such as "relevance," "competence," "experience," "efficiency," "coherency," "excellence"—words that give the appearance of importance.

- Business-speak considers grammar a relic of the past. It misuses circumlocution, distends syntax, mistreats words, and decks itself out in a gaudy array of technical and managerial terms. It corrupts language in masterly fashion: the business world loves malapropisms. For example, when you "decline" a logo, a message, or a value, you are not turning it down but merely adopting it for other uses, featured below. Nouns are turned into verbs as in "to access," or "to migrate" personnel from one department to another; intransitive verbs become transitive, as in "growing one's business."

- The language of business expresses the politics of an impersonal power. It seeks neither to convince nor to prove, or even to seduce, but offers obvious statements in a uniform fashion without any value judgments. The goal? To make you obey. Beware: Joseph Goebbels, Hitler's right-hand man, once said, "We don't speak to communicate anything but to create a certain effect." And in fact, business newspeak is halfway between self-proclaimed scientific objectivity and the peremptory stridency of the slogan. Thus we get: "Interdepartmental cooperation *must* be optimized." "It is *imperative* that the new modus operandi be achieved by the deadline of the fifteenth." Or: "Implementing the orientations defined by the project *are* and *will remain* a priority."

- Business-speak takes only the most well-traveled roads, where every twist and turn is familiar.

Even if a text or memo says nothing, it can still be decoded: it reveals its meaning whenever it diverges from the secret code. Every deviation from the expected reveals something. So if you have nothing better to do, you can become an expert in jargon. . . .

This language has a hold over us and claims to speak for us, reducing the employee to a simple piece of machinery. Get up, machine, and get to work! Your perceptions, your feelings, your ambition, must be translatable into spreadsheets and graphs, and your labor is but a "process" that must be rationalized.

Corrupting language is a costly affair. Our words seem to have been doctored. When it becomes difficult to disentangle truth and lies and to quash rumors, mistrust reigns. Not surprisingly, employees become paranoid that a vast plot is being hatched against them by top management. It's true: the bosses speak a language worthy of *Pravda,* the Soviet organ of official truth. But does this really mean they're up to no good? Sometimes it does, but sometimes there is a more innocent explanation: executives speak newspeak because they've been trained to, and they are chosen for certain positions of power on the basis of their mastery of this lingua franca. Jargonism is in their blood.

A training course in "native language" would be helpful in a number of our executive suites, but this is rarely on the syllabus of the executive MBA. They prefer neurolinguistic programming (NLP) and similarly half-baked approaches, whose primary objective is to keep everyone thinking and speaking in circles.

Acronyms: A Thicket, a Wilderness, Nay, a Veritable Labyrinth

If the newspeak of the business world is particularly repulsive, it is also because everybody speaks in abbreviations. While jargon has eliminated a certain number of words, it has also created a large number of them—especially those based on abbreviations and contractions—without a thought for how awful they sound. The names of units, groups, and departments are always acronyms. This is the sort of thing one hears at a meeting: "AGIR has become IPN, which supervises the STI, divesting the SSII of control of the DM, but the latter will waste no time in subsuming RTI." One hour of this sort of talk in the cafeteria is enough to drive you batty. The objective is to make those who know what the acronyms mean think that they belong to the privileged few, an inner circle who really knows what's what.

There's no point, however, in memorizing the meaning of these cryptic acronyms. They're changing all the time, in accordance with the successive restructurings aimed at reshuffling the cards without ever changing the deck—anything but! What this proliferation of abbreviations shows is that over the course of the many reorganizations and mergers/acquisitions, businesses become so complex and labyrinthine that you don't know whether you are coming or going. As a result, competition intensifies, responsibilities overlap, Russian dolls multiply. A progressive financial daily* summed up the phenomenon as follows: "We belong to the era of multiple cross-

*A fine example of oxymoron. As the reader will gather later on, this is my favorite type of style (see also "Corporate Culture: *Culture,* My Ass").

world ownership." Translation in plain talk: "The organization is a shambles."

There is a golden rule in the process of naming teams: each unit is named in such a way as to imply that its importance is vital to the firm, without being too explicit about what it actually does for fear of creating too much work. Most acronyms are formed with the same words, which include the following: "information," "technology," "support," "management," "development," "application," "data," "service," "direction," "center," "computer," "network," "research," "raccoon," "market," "product," "marketing," "consumer," and "client." You have one minute to find the one that doesn't belong in this list. . .

Foreign Languages: *No Pasarán*

Nevertheless, even though it's hard for them, the French have to admit that the Americans are the masters of capitalism. Harvard is the Bethlehem of money. So you have to listen to what Uncle Sam has to say on the matter. The business schools of Western Europe suffer from an inferiority complex vis-à-vis their American models. No sooner does a word become all the rage in the United States than it crosses the Atlantic like a wave and engulfs our management schools, our commercial institutions, and our businessmen's speech. Linguistic inaccuracies are irrelevant; it's enough to sprinkle these buzzwords over the transparencies and "charts." That's the basic idea.

Here is a sample of contemporary business French; the italicized words are in English in the original: "I'm doing the *follow-up* on a *merging project* with a *coach;* I'm *checking* the *downsizing.*" This means you're firing people. Similarly, "reengineering" has taken the place of "reorganizing." And when the French terms have so negative a connotation that they become unusable, English is used as a practical cosmetic measure: in the hush-hush environment of the firm, one must *remain positive* even when everything is going wrong. You've been fired? Smile and say *"cheese"*!

This relationship of fascination/repulsion with regard to the United States explains why no one in France really speaks the language of these barbarians. It's a known fact that the French are not very good at immersing themselves in the fine points of English. And we're not talking here about the language of Shakespeare, a difficult author writing in an archaic style, but rather of Michael Jackson, a singer who has more shades of white and gray in his makeup drawer than he has words in his vocabulary.

French executives, who are supposed to be able to communicate with the whole world within the framework of flexible, cosmopolitan networks, are irremediably bad in languages. Is it because of their chauvinistic resistance to globalization? Could they possibly believe that the business world of the future will speak French, which for them (and them alone) is the most precise and beautiful language in the world? To speak a no-man's-language in the workplace is already enough of a chore; no point in making it more complicated by learning English. . . .

Platitudes Aplenty

The rash of platitudes and commonplaces bandied about in the business world, which can't get enough of them, is flabbergasting. Conventional turns of phrase and old chestnuts abound. In fact, only the most conventional and hackneyed expressions find their way into the comforting, cliché-ridden world of the office; the jokey "Damn the torpedoes," so *yesterday,* and the enigmatic and disturbing "What goes around comes around" are scarcely worth mentioning. But the point, of course, is to "dumb things down," as they say at the office.

The newcomer to the business world is perplexed until he understands that the impersonal appearance of this half-baked wisdom hides nothing more than the interests and ambitions of the person voicing them. In the treasury of commonly used proverbs and expressions, the following are particular favorites (with the translation in parentheses):

"There are no problems, there are only solutions" (an absurd sentence, greatly appreciated by engineers justifying their existence).

"Knowledge is power" (which means: "I know more than you").

"Work less but work smarter" (slogan used by the most hypocritical bosses to make you get to work).

"It's all a matter of organization" (same meaning as above).

"You have to prioritize" ("It's out of the question for me to work harder").

"The sky's the limit" ("I can't stand it anymore").

"Where there's smoke there's fire" ("I smell a rat").

"Let's not beat around the bush" ("I'm going to be frank: no more hypocrisy").

Taking notes in meetings is never futile for the lover of empty phrases and nonsense. And then, every so often (anything can happen), the great, generous womb of language yields up a pearl, an unexpected or pleasant turn of phrase, which makes up for all those afternoons spent listening to garbage.

II.

The Dice Are Loaded

In the great game of business, it's your corporation that makes the moves. You are a mere pawn and your job is its gift to you. You say "Yes, sir" and "No, sir," act politely and obediently and don't raise your voice, but wait quietly for your paycheck at the end of the month. If you think you are "proving yourself," impressing them with your "training," or "making yourself indispensable" to your boss, you must have come through the wrong door. You're there to sell yourself and to make them buy, not to "open your big mouth" (as they say in meetings when people let themselves go a bit), because that's the best way to "be given your walking papers."

Money Costs More Than You Think

Everyone works for money, and for the tons of things you can buy with it. Money is the lifeblood of business, but you can't say so. That's taboo. Corporations never actually mention "money"; that would be vulgar. They prefer such words as "turnover," "profit," "salary," "revenue," "budget," "premium," and "savings," all much more refined. One day, in the middle of a meeting on motivation, I dared to say that the only reason I came to work was to put food on the table. There were fifteen seconds of absolute silence, and everyone seemed uncomfortable. Even though the French word for work, *"travail,"* etymologically derives from an instrument of torture, it's imperative to let it be known, no matter the circumstance, that you are working *because you are interested in your work*. Even when put on the rack for hours on end by your pitiless jailers, you'd better not say otherwise.

Furthermore, you chose this line of work. What better proof that it's intrinsically "worthwhile"? But for whom? Worthwhile for you, or worthwhile for your firm? That's the million-dollar question. . . . And if you didn't choose this line of work, it chose you. When you come right down to it, do we really choose anything in life? Our partner? Our religion? Our analyst? Our life? So what's the problem? But let's leave aside such existential questions, which don't belong here (although we shouldn't forget them too much, since they are essential in working out what we really want, which should have some value, after all). In short, you work because you have to, since no one likes to work! If people liked it so much, they would work for free!

People have a passion for money. All you have to do is look at the number of special issues that business magazines are always publishing on the essential topic of insatiable curiosity: executives' salaries. Knowing how much other people make allows you to compare yourself to your neighbor, which is always interesting. But the peanuts you gather each month serve mostly to acquire a lot of amusing gadgets. Having a Treo smartphone—a PDA and a cell phone all in one—makes up for a lot. For the middle manager, the question is not so much Hamlet's "To be or not to be?" as it is "To be or to have?" That's the real question. At least the average manager of today isn't as miserable as Shakespeare's unfortunate hero. Although, sometimes, I wonder.

They Tell You to Succeed

I'm successful in business
I'm successful in love
I change secretaries often
I look down from above . . .

croons the businessman in the popular hit "Businessman's Blues." But why is he unhappy, this poor devil, who's rolling in dough—and who regrets only the fact that he's not an artist? Maybe because he's working himself into the ground for a derisory piece of fat, and the fact that other people envy his salary. The driving force of success is competition with others: as Sigmund Freud pointed out, it is nothing more than the narcissistic quest to stand out from the crowd, if only in some minuscule way.

Hence the importance of status symbols in the corporate world. Hence the importance of the office, allocated according to rank. For example, at level *x* you occupy a sixty-square-foot partitioned office that you share with an intern or a colleague, while at level *x*+1 you get a real office measuring seventy square feet with—take note—a little round table used for meetings. At *x*+2 you are given a nice set of wooden office furniture: absolute, irrefutable proof that your firm loves you more than some of your less fortunate colleagues. And this is terribly important. Funny how love is all that matters. . . .

But, try as he might to rise in the ranks and amass ever more gadgets and tangible signs of success, the middle manager is doomed to remain just that. Once an office rat, always an office rat. The positions of "great responsibility" (company officers, executive director, department head) are monopolized by graduates of the leading business schools. These people are technocrats like you but at a higher level, since they reap untold benefits from the "network" that is created by fraternities, family connections, the "right" schools. The middle manager is a product of the middle class; the high-level exec is cut from a different cloth. He is as far from the middle manager as the latter is from the part-timers and temps, who have very few rights and are but one step away from being unemployed.

Those of us who have no connections and no one to light a fire under us have no choice but to play a role and go through the motions. This is why clothes are so important in the corporate world: they help define just what is expected from the middle manager—who is, of course, healthy, athletic, communicative, enterprising, ambitious, optimistic, with an aura of informality and professionalism, of masculinity (or femininity) and sober conservatism. The "dress code"' is precisely that: the business suit is mandatory for both women and men in most economic sectors, except on "casual Fridays," when one has the "right" to dress differently from the first four days of the week. Friday clothes are appropriate for this day alone and, small wonder, are hardly the clothes that you yourself would wear if you wanted to relax (that would be too simple). Your only freedom is your choice of tie and socks.

How long will we have to wait for "dress-up Mondays" and "cross-dress Thursdays," just to complicate things a little more? How long before the office begins to resemble a royal reception, where a horde of fluttering, idle courtiers are hanging on the king's every word, not trying to accomplish anything but simply looking fabulous?

Power Struggles: Watch Your Back

In the struggle between the corporation and you, the corporation wins, just as in the jungle the lion usually gets the better of the antelope. This might seem self-evident, but the official line is quite different: that in today's corporate world all conflicts are resolved through rational discourse, negotiations, and an egalitarian contract in which everyone comes out a winner. Nobody's fooled by this fantasy, especially when it comes to employees' pay. Salaries are determined by a highly unequal power relationship in a "free" market that pits a sole wage earner who needs to work against a highly structured business ready to take advantage of every loophole in employment regulations.

Business is only interested in employees' "right to work" in order to, well, circumvent it. It pounces on every chance to create temporary positions, hire freelancers, and encourage flexible hours while slowly paring back the mechanics of job security set in place over a century of labor struggle. This allows a company to "keep its hands free" and to avoid making any long-term commitments to its employees. Thus the creation of a double workforce. Stable, qualified workers, on the one hand, enjoy quite high salaries, relative job security, real social protection, and certain "advantages" (various kinds of vouchers, vacation camps for their children, special prices, housing accommodations, etc.). These are the people with cushy jobs. On the other hand, part-timers and contractual workers make up a workforce that is less qualified, underpaid, and less protected than the first. To these hired hands the corporation is under no obligation to provide health insurance or job training. Officially they perform minor services, but in fact they often tackle the work that the first, more affluent group does not want to do. If you're going to have slackers, somebody has to do the work! Things have been this way since time immemorial, so it won't change overnight. Perhaps it's the only real universal law: for there to be masters, there must be slaves; for there to be rich, there must be poor. At every opportunity, the strong continue to crush the weak, the superior to dominate the inferior. To make sure things are perfectly clear, repeat after me, all together: *That's just the way it is and, in any case, "there is no alternative."* At least, that's what they want us to believe.

One of the commonest forms of injustice inside the corporation is psychological harassment. This is the treatment that for too long has remain unacknowledged: the secretary who is treated like a doormat, the junior staffer who is pressured and treated like dirt by a manipulative manager who counts on the weaker party's silent obedience. Any protection is at once real and illusory because, no matter what course is taken, what legal sanctions are sought, and what rights are asserted, most employees fail to see their personal dignity satisfied. It's enough to make you think that our dissatisfaction with life is absolutely fundamental.

Ever more rights, ever less satisfaction. The idea's not new: the Rolling Stones were singing about it when our parents were young.

What's the origin of violence in the workplace, directed against specially chosen victims? Since most managers want the same thing (a company car, a higher rank on the corporate ladder, appointment to a superimportant decision-making committee), competition is stiff, which threatens the cohesion of the group as a whole. This rivalry creates conflicts that can be resolved only when a scapegoat emerges from the ranks. Such is the theory of the philosopher René Girard, who believes that communities sacrifice one of their own to ensure the unity of the group.

And speaking of strengthening the morale of a group of wage earners, I have an iconoclastic suggestion that pesters me every time I participate in a boring meeting that lasts a little too long (which is often). Why not take it out on the CEO? Kidnapping your boss and cutting off his head might seem unthinkable, but then, who would have imagined, before 1789, that a king could be guillotined? France's history is colorful and inspired; let's tip our hats to it by organizing a remake of its finest hours! Off with their heads! Sacrificing a chief executive would allow us to reengineer the corporate pact; to rethink the relationships between executives and middle managers, between the upper echelons and the base; to reflect upon the redistribution of labor, offices, salaries, etc.

Degrees and Diplomas: Or, How to Make Paper Airplanes

Too many diplomas is like no diplomas at all. The more there are, the less they're worth. Need proof that your diplomas are no longer worth much? Well, whatever the paper you use as a fig leaf, the corporate world merely tolerates your presence; what's more, in the fertile 1990s, it developed the concept of "nomadic offices." This system consists of allocating office space to people as they show up for work. Thus, the middle manager, who does not have a permanent workstation, is always "an outsider," making it out of the question for him to put down roots. A marvelous inversion arises from this state of affairs: the employee is no longer someone who makes him- or herself useful to others; it's the corporation that makes itself useful by *allowing* employees to work, granting them this precious opportunity to work.

The philosopher Hannah Arendt once noted that capitalism creates the superfluous. Well, now *we* are what's most superfluous! And we live in a world of excess: too many kinds of coffee, too many magazines, too many types of bread, too many digital recordings of Beethoven's Ninth, too many choices of rearview mirrors on the latest Renault. Sometimes you say to yourself: It's too much, it's all too much. . . .

But don't throw away your diplomas yet. They may not measure intelligence or competence, but at least documents are proof that the wage earner, the small-time manager, knows how to buckle down. Only a former student who was able to tolerate years of study, the stupidity of his teachers, the pressure of friends to do what everyone else is doing, is capable of putting up with the banality and repetitiveness of thirty-odd years in an office! Because that's what they expect from you, now that most jobs no longer require a high level of technical or intellectual skill. They involve routine above all, and require so little initiative or inventive spirit that whoever completes the required level of study is already overqualified for most of the available positions.

It's enough to be mediocre. "As part of a small team of specialists, you won't have any say in personnel decisions or any operational role in restructuring or development. Since you have no solid foundation in economics or finance, no significant experience in the fields of capital investment or mergers/acquisition—neither of which you have ever heard of—you won't need any outstanding personal motivation in order to form a lasting partnership," mocks Laurent Laurent in his ironic *Six mois au fond d'un bureau* (*Six Months Buried in an Office*).

Whether you're a shrinking violet or an airhead, you have every chance of getting ahead in the regulated universe of big business. The corporate world doesn't discriminate.

Employment and Employability: Knowing How to Brand™ and Sell Oneself

Would the company that insists "Our people are our most precious asset" lie to us? The statement is troubling: Stalin used to say it. Does this mean that the more you value human beings, the more you oppress them in real life? Businesses take what they need and discard the rest. Unemployment affects all social classes. The ranks of young and unqualified workers that once made up the bulk of the unemployed are now being joined by skilled supervisors, technicians, and managers. The promise of upward mobility once offered by business has become a reality of downward mobility. The only advantage, for the time being, is that things are still moving (see the section titled "Mobility: Journey to the End of Your Career")—but not in the right direction. The moral of the story is that in business, even when there's nothing to hope for, there's always something to fear.

Businesses demand a lot but are careful not to

promise too much, with no long-term guarantees. Why bother? Promises, as we all know, are meant only for those who listen to them. Moreover, in a world where opportunity is supposed to be equal, the unemployed *must* be unemployed for a reason. If you find yourself out of a job, it's because you're not as good as those who still have jobs. If your position is eliminated, it's because you didn't prove its usefulness: you didn't know how to make the most of your responsibilities, how to interest clients, etc. There's no getting around it: it's all your fault! And what makes your failure worse is that we live in a world in which work is the principal way of defining our identities. Work, work, work: that's the standing order. Since we still have a semblance of common sense and free will, we are entitled to ask: What for?

To keep from being unemployed, you have to cultivate your "employability." The wage earner needs this ill-defined yet indispensable quality these days, at a time when even a product as ordinary as sliced bread vaunts its "toastability," its "butterability," and—why not?—even its "marmaladability," in order to seduce consumers who never knew that this is what they wanted. Perhaps we should review the employability of the word "employability." It really means nothing more than the ability to convince others that one is worth employing! And why do they need to be convinced? Because now that everyone is interchangeable, the middle manager needs to try to stand out from the rest. How? Well, through your personality. The golden rule for recruitment can be summed up in a single sentence: Today people are hired not for what they know how to do but for what they are. Interpersonal and communication skills are paramount; technical know-how and qualifications are mere accessories. Soon we'll be teaching people only how to seduce the recruiters. Workers with nothing to recommend you, welcome.

So you have to be your own salesperson, to "sell yourself" as if your personality were a product with a market value. For Tom Peters,* pompous guru of the new economy, to succeed you need to see yourself as a commercial venture: the brand *You*. The objective is to make it known that you know how to make things known; do this, and there will always be time later to

*Author of the work *Liberation Management* (New York: Knopf, 1992)—another oxymoron! Needless to say, I don't recommend it.

show whether you actually know how to do anything. Try a little harder and you, too, can be like the hero of the film *Jerry Maguire,* in which we see Tom Cruise work into the early hours drafting memos on the need to espouse novelty, for being present on the Web under pain of losing social status, for launching this or that advertising campaign in a trendier fashion.

Image counts more than product, seduction more than production, because the average manager, hired for his flexibility and malleability, serves his company by selling *what*? Mass-produced, standardized goods, first and foremost, often manufactured in third world countries; any old Chinese worker can make them, and the less added value the article has, the more persuasion is needed to convince the consumer of its merit. Then there are the products that are a little harder to manufacture, for which we invented *marketing*—a bazaar ethology that lets you know what you don't need and how someone can sell it to you anyway. Last, and most important, there are services that, for many, are far from essential. Here the seller has to do his job well because if he doesn't, the buyer might realize that nothing but hot air is being sold.

Individual attention to the client and personalized

service aim at nothing more than reintroducing a note of reality into a capitalist mode of production that has been completely eliminated. It's the "something extra," the "personal touch" so lacking in a standardized world. The business world thus mimics an authenticity it has done everything in its power to crush under the steamroller of mass production, training its employees to make the bogus look authentic.

And that, indeed, is what we're here for. We were awarded our diplomas in order to become the acceptable faces of our companies—and only secondarily because we are intelligent. If that does sometimes happen, it is by accident.

The Defeat of the Word

There are fewer and fewer conflicts in the workplace; the number of strike days annually is on the decline. Order reigns in the factories, in the cubicled "open-space" offices. But how can we rebel against ideas that are so slippery to grab hold of? How do you stand up against "modernity," "autonomy," "transparency," or "conviviality"? How do you confront powers and institutions that ceaselessly repeat that they are there only to "keep up with the times" and do their best to respond to "popular demand" and the "needs of the individual"?

In theory, everyone can say what he or she thinks. The boss's door is always open; everyone is free to go and speak to him. We're all on a first-name basis, and your manager often assumes the role of kindly leader, pal, or even psychoanalyst. Why not? Once or twice a year, the employee "evaluates his own performance," which results in an "overall assessment." How can employees granted the right to evaluate themselves and others ever make common cause against the hierarchy? Yes, you're free to talk, but there's the catch: you can talk as much as you like and nothing will ever change. Talk is cheap and costs the company nothing.

In France, the exercise of power is as centralized as possible. Rarely are decisions made collectively. Companies hate doing anything face-to-face and avoid any discussion that allows the different parties to participate: that might lead to compromise. The language of business is a one-way street that contorts normal speech and thwarts any possibility of response. Communication is short-circuited, and the employee has no voice. And if a genuine public outburst ever did occur, wouldn't that upset the French values of good taste, moderation, and propriety?

When a decision is "made," the power structure is so opaque that it is impossible to see where it came from. Who decided? Nobody knows. Is there an inspired and benevolent Being who decides in favor of the common good? No, but enough people believe there is, which helps to lend this hypothetical character substance. And He's the reason we give up our rights as responsible employees! Great Being on high, thy will be done. . . .

Since words are inconsequential, all that's left is the harmless pleasure of speaking ill of others. Many revel in petty rivalries and conflicts, deriving great satisfaction from undermining their colleagues or criticizing the firm. It's all mumble and grumble, as General de Gaulle once put it.

Faced with this failure of language, what can the unions do? It's their job, after all, to create dialogue. Big companies like Wal-Mart have succeeded in circumventing them. It's easy to see why. This is quite understandable. The new deal put forward by the "new management" leaves them baffled and irrelevant. There is no place for them in it. In fact, they are seen as dinosaurs left over from a hierarchical and bureaucratic world that has had its day but is still hanging on. Moreover, the unions are all run by people who were student activists in the 1960s; if they had succeeded in changing anything, we would have noticed. Thus, the unionist is often a disillusioned fifty-year-old who deplores the inertia and lack of "fighting spirit" of today's youth.

The Planned Obsolescence of the Worker

The religion of the corporate world is novelty. What is new is always right. Young people inject fresh blood into the organization. Any firm that panics at the idea of not being cutting-edge is keen to hire them. Of course, it's really society as a whole that peddles this image of the fresh and healthy young people living life to the max.

The young have the advantage of not having love handles; they can wear slim-cut suits and breeze into the work world without a care in the world. They think that such words as "proactive" and "benchmarking" actually mean something, believe that the sacrosanct injunction "Be autonomous!" is meant to be taken at face value, hope to see their merits recognized, and expect, well, to be loved. Ah, youth! "Young people" are all the more precious to the firm because it expects everything and its opposite from them: that they keep their mouths shut and stick up for themselves; listen quietly and come up with all the ideas; fit in and stand out in the crowd. . . . It's a bit like being a child. The parents want the little dears to respect them and be like them, but at the same time hope that their children will succeed where the fathers and mothers failed—two completely incompatible expectations.

It's another story altogether for "seniors." Historically (see "Employment and Employability: Knowing How to Brand™ and Sell Oneself"), corporate restructuring or budget-slashing layoffs have primarily affected workers aged fifty and over. Fifty-year-olds, out! These kinds of cutbacks were facilitated by the implementation, during the seventies and eighties, by early retirement plans and severance pay programs. The upshot is that in France today, only one-third of men ages fifty-five to sixty-four work: a world record. Getting rid of "old" workers is a clever way of weeding out potential sources of opposition: the fifty-year-old is less flexible than the thirty-year-old who has just landed his first stable job and who has been told that he's been earmarked for a great future with the company.

In short, you're washed-up in business at an age when in politics you're considered a whippersnapper or even a young Turk. Washed up at the age when Cézanne painted admirable paintings of *Le Mont Sainte-Victoire*, or when Dostoyevsky wrote *The Brothers Karamazov.* The middle manager's "shelf life"—to use a term much appreciated by consultants and generally applied to products—is short. There is but one step from the "rise to power" (up until the age of thirty, sometimes longer) to the decline (starting at age forty-five). All it takes to be thrown from the Capitoline to the Tarpeian Rock is a single flourish of the human resources administrator's pen.

But this planned obsolescence of the worker cannot last forever, since the combined interests of the firm and the individual employees, both inclined toward early retirement, are in total contradiction with those of an aging society, which has fewer and fewer young workers to finance the retirement of its seniors. Since this issue is a powder keg, one will see many a fine display of social fireworks in the near future.

III.

The Biggest Rip-offs

Managers and employees, you're being lied to. Don't be fooled. The firm is telling fibs that are also traps: let's defuse them together. The dictates of mobility, the endlessly repetitive talk about mobility, ethics, the new information and communications technologies—it's all so much claptrap.

Mobility: Journey to the End of Your Career

Mobility is the closest a middle manager gets to a religious truth; it's the only one available to him. At a time when society as a whole has no idea where it's going, the employee is being asked to "project himself positively into the future." Do you feel like a mercenary in the world in which you move, commandeered by causes you do not espouse, and continuously sent by these causes to places foreign to you? No matter: "Life is what you make it," you're told time and time again. And mobility is a categorical imperative for a capitalist system whose ultimate aim is to make the useless both indispensable and expendable—and the quicker the better.

François Salvaing, in his book *La boîte* (*The Firm*), gives us an example of a typical conversation between an employee and his boss:

> "What's your idea of a career?" asks William Leveque [the new director of human resources, formerly in the automobile industry].
>
> "Three years per position."
>
> "Why is that?"
>
> "Any more than that, you get stuck in a rut, and people think you're dead in the water. Less than that, you can't get to the bottom of things: you don't know the ocean, only the waves."

Move on! Three years at the parent firm, two years in Singapore to oversee a subsidiary, three years in Backwaterville for management control. Your support structure will follow; it goes without saying that in the name of sacrosanct mobility, your children and spouse will enthusiastically move and abandon their routines, friends, and jobs and fall right in line. And if by chance they don't follow, change your spouse; clearly the current one is not mobile enough to keep up with your skyrocketing career. The CEOs set the example, but on a grander scale: these high-tech nomads shuttle between multinationals or big businesses, staying a few years at each job and receiving en route signing bonuses and golden parachutes in the millions.

It's a proven fact that everything can be bought and sold, including human resources. The Marquis de Sade imagined a sexual utopia in which everyone had the right to possess whoever they liked; human beings, reduced to their sexual organs, would thus become strictly anonymous and interchangeable. Of course de Sade was an aristocrat, the last of his line, and depraved, but nowadays each of us is an object of exchange, destined to be placed and displaced at the whim of the firm. And for the firm, the human animal—constrained by experience, slowed down by training, worn-out by repetition, weighed down by influences of culture and climate—is a design malfunction. How heavy is human clay! It hinders the scenario of global mobility that business tries to impose on us.

It's true that our middle manager is an obstruction. Professionally he is hardly flexible, afraid of being demoted and being forced to take on a task beneath him. This obsession with rank, privilege, and prerogatives feeds corporate behavior, caste arrogance, and the endless squabbling over precedence. All this baggage makes a middle manager unmanageable.

The dream of most managers is not to have to move every three years but rather to buy a little house in an unassuming residential suburb, then later on, as he moves up the property ladder, the house that shows that they've finally "made it." Once in debt for twenty years to acquire his "home sweet home," he doesn't want to move anymore.

Our service-sector slave can thus be "mobile" without moving, since our modern megacorporations can offer countless opportunities. If he's lucky, he can restrict his mobility to changes in skyscrapers or transfers from one floor to another: you can begin your career on the twenty-first floor of 201 East Fiftieth Street, then get sent over to the fourth floor of 299 Park Avenue, before being transferred to the twenty-first floor of 1745 Broadway, then move back to headquarters at 1540 Broadway, before taking your well-earned retirement. Mobility is tiring!

Corporate Culture: *Culture,* My Ass!

The word "culture" was introduced to the corporate world about twenty years ago. Michel Houellebecq wrote ironically in *Whatever*: "Long before the phrase was fashionable, my firm developed a true corporate *culture* (with the creation of a logo, the distribution of sweatshirts to the employees, seminars on motivation in Turkey). It's a productive business, enjoying an enviable reputation in its field. It is, in every sense, a success."

Culture, which by definition serves no purpose, has now found a role as the consort of business. Right off the bat we have a beached whale, since there is nothing that disdains culture as much as business does.

"Corporate culture" is therefore an oxymoron, a stylistic turn of phrase created by associating two words that have no business being together. And although company executives like the phrase when everything is going well, as it creates an artificial feeling of identity and belonging, when things go wrong it's perceived as an archaism that thwarts change.

In fact, "corporate culture" is nothing more than the crystallization of the stupidity of a group of people at a given moment. This pseudopatriotism is made up of a dense mass of slightly stale habits, aptitudes, and sartorial and behavioral tics that verge on caricature. Rewritten by the managers, it becomes the official line, with heroes and celebrations designed to motivate the worker and encourage identification with a unified, tight-knit firm. It translates into an orgy of vapid seminars, unwearable T-shirts, badges (yes, they still exist), and so-called motivational slogans.

Why all the knickknacks and buzzwords? Because business, like society as a whole, feels threatened by the rumblings of fragmentation. The most pressing question today for the community, be it nation or company, is "How can we all live together?"—a question to which there are fewer and fewer answers. Modern philosophers like Jürgen Habermas and John Rawls have exhausted themselves trying to find one. Companies don't have any more of a clue than the community at large as to how to hold things together; their response is to create a "big family" by producing signs and symbols with which its employees are supposed to identify.

Let it burn itself out. The day when the company has no other purpose than to create logos and jingles for its employees will be the day the company will put itself out of business. In the meantime, we just have to find the courage to keep getting up every morning for something that makes no sense at all to us, and this is very hard indeed.

Ethics, Schmethics

As goodness marches on, hand in hand with ecological correctness and moral irreproachability, business cannot escape from the spate of fine sentiments and the tidal wave of universal charity, obligatory idealism, unwavering solidarity, and universal human rights flooding the far corners of the globe. So it adopted "ethics," which is nothing more than a substitute for morals. This product has invaded the workplace through all the redrafted charters and codes that confusedly set forth fundamental principles, values, and rules of behavior. Ethics is a detergent word, used time and time again to clean consciences without scrubbing.

This new knee-jerk ethics dons various hats, such as "corporate social responsibility" and "sustained development." Both are oxymorons (already defined in the previous section, "Corporate Culture: *Culture,* My Ass!"). Contradiction in terms or not, what business today is not "concerned" about the greenhouse effect and the holes in the ozone layer? The problem is that ethics is a bit like culture: the less one has, the more one flaunts it—so much of the talk about ethics is already suspect. Besides, in the oil industry, Shell occupies first place among the "ethically correct." Shell, humanistic? It's doubtful, but the board of directors of the most profitable group in Europe is certainly convinced that morality pays. Beware of the gangster in Boy Scout's clothing. . . .

Ethics proves that business can make anything profitable—even things that undermine profit—with ethics at the top of the list. While business absorbs and deforms everything at hand, its customs and "values" gush forth, spread, and discolor everything like an oil slick. Hospitals have caught the managerial virus: their vocabulary is punctuated with such terms as "market niches," "productivity potential," and "clientele." Schools are infected, too: "skill assessments" figure more and more prominently in "new business plans" that everyone hopes will translate into "goal-oriented agreements" with the students. Business and its logic of productivity have become the reference point in a society that thinks *marketing* every time it opens its mouth.

The proof? The excessive use of the verb "to manage." In business language it means the administration of people and things, but it has slipped into every aspect of existence. The Socialists manage their defeat, women their divorces, the athlete his injuries, the Olympic medalist his success, the doctor his clientele, each of us his or her sexuality. Let me manage you, my little serf!

The Strategy: The Art of Appearing Smarter Than You Are

"Strategy." There, the great word has been spoken. One need only utter it to have the impression of entering the holy of holies. The word itself, which comes from the vocabulary of warfare and refers to a gamut of available tactics, has no specific content. After an in-depth study of the issue, I declare that in fact there are only two possible strategies: refocusing on basic skills (what the company already knows how to do) and diversification (what the company does not yet understand but will have to learn, since "it's not good to have all your eggs in the same basket"). Strategy is simple, because there are only two choices. As Fidel Castro once put it in one of his torrential speeches from the good old days, "There is no third way."

Let's look at our second lesson in strategy: when a company diversifies, the policies are always justified by the "synergies" between the "core business" and the new activities. Synergies between two different businesses, like the "chemistry" shared by a couple, are often insufficient reason to keep the two together. Strategy involves as much guesswork as clairvoyance. As Scott Adams rails in his hard-hitting *Dogbert's Top Secret Management Handbook*, "Corporate strategy is defined as all the stuff you've already done plus all the good stuff your competitors are doing."

Strategy has the merit of engendering countless memos written in zesty jargon. In the French business where I work, which operates in the field of energy, I recently read a priceless piece of gobbledygook drawn up by consultants:

> Remaining a *leader* implies securing the *sourcing* and/or the positioning of the group in the gas-market *mainstream* as well as identifying with a *mix/portfolio* of optimal production as a function of the *mass market*. This distances us from the *pure-player* model, which had previously led us to outline a *package offer*. Internally, the corporate management must be carried out in voluntary fashion over the interbranch network, thanks to catch-ups from the *bottom up*. The

> PMT missions will be defined in accordance with the gaps between the consolidated image and the 2006 target.

That was worth chopping down trees for, wasn't it?

Such absurdities prove that strategy is not formulated by people who are more intelligent than you. So, then, who draws it up? It is either decided upon by an expert group of parasites (advisers, right-hand men, consultants) or concocted by one person alone, the boss. The first solution, for all its inefficiency, is preferable to the second: it sometimes prevents huge blunders. And we've got some fine examples of huge blunders that have been made here in France. You'd think, in fact, we were cursed. In 1992, Crédit Lyonnais foundered in near bankruptcy after a foolhardy expansion that was supposed to make it the number-one bank in the world. Ten years later, here we go again: in 2002, Vivendi's financial crisis led to a fire sale on the mirages of the new economy, and the company was forced to shelve its attempt to become the number two worldwide in media and telecommunications.

In both cases, the deposed CEOs (Jean-Yves

Haberer and Jean-Marie Messier, respectively) were graduates of the best schools in France. In both cases, these men thought that the acquisition of a studio in Hollywood (MGM for one and Universal for the other) would be a profitable diversification. After all, a simple bank with tellers' windows or a useful but filthy waste-processing center are too boring! But Hollywood proved to be a key factor in their downfalls. It's hardly surprising that corporate executives would crave glitz and jewels: Where else would one find the glamour that is absent in corporate life?

Strategy, for some enlightened beings, is a kind of magic wand, capable of changing a frog into a prince—or is it the other way around?

New Information and Communications Technologies Are the Wave of the Future

Computers are the wave of the future. People were already saying this in the 1970s. The latest information and communications technologies are the offspring of computers and the Internet. For twenty years now, corporations have been investing hand over fist in these technologies, hoping for phenomenal gains in productivity: computers are everywhere; the Internet will change the world, create jobs, usher in a period of intense growth. All problems will be solved with the Internet; it will revolutionize human history. With this marvelous communication tool, problems of frontier, race, and religion will disappear. The Internet will open up the backwaters, reduce the gap between the haves and the have-nots in society, encourage north-south exchanges, educate the illiterate, teach children, and liberate the housewife. We shall all be brothers and sisters, there will be no more war, all together now . . .

The song sounds sweet, but the reality is more brutal. For the time being, the only undeniable effect of the white tornado of the computer sciences has been the massive elimination of secretarial jobs, which were in fact quite useful. Anything else? No, but these new technologies have definitely increased the productivity of none other than the computer and telecommunications sector, according to Robert M. Solow, Nobel Prize recipient in economics. That's rich.

But the new information and communications

technologies, without having given proof positive of their usefulness, have at least created something concrete: a language, and that's not nothing. It's an abstruse language, for the geeks and nerds speak a jargon understood only by initiates: discussions of different development platforms or the choice of the most appropriate software solution, all of it studded with gems like "html," "xml," "Dreamweaver," and "ColdFusion." Here's one example, sent to me by a friend who does understand what it all means:

> The merging of WSFL and Xlang is just as important as the two new protocols. The main interest of Web services, as much inside as outside the firewall, resides in the rapid development of the XML ad hoc applications. BPEL4WS will offer a more standardized method to achieve the same goal, simply by fusing two already known languages. But it seems that the development initiatives overlooked various operational front-end B2B processing protocols, notably the ebXML protocol, the BPML [business process modeling] language and the wholly new WSCI [Web services choreography interface].

I imagine some readers will have fallen asleep in their chairs. What does it all mean? When you read such a sentence, you feel stupid. That's probably what it's there for: to make us recognize our inferiority. It's all incomprehensible, and it's incomprehensible that it should be incomprehensible to us, since we do know how to use the Internet! After all, we spend hours of office time trying to find important information on the average water temperature at a Caribbean resort, or on fly-fishing in Montana.

IV.

The Idiots You Rub Shoulders With

Since I don't want to get in trouble with my colleagues, this chapter requires a disclaimer. Françoise Vernay, a famous publisher, once remarked that in business one finds the same percentage of reputable people as anywhere else. And I've noticed that this is true. Here I'm simply making fun of certain types and caricatures who, it's clear, are barely worth the trouble.

The Average Manager: Presentable and Preferably Male

The ranks of the middle managers are made up of very average men, a species described with verve by Pierre Dac: "The average Frenchman is an invertebrate mammal whose distinguishing feature is to have no distinguishing features. He professes first and foremost complete faith in the officially established order and morality; his driver's license bears more or less the following description: height: average; brow: average; eyes: indeterminate; nose: average; chin: oval; distinguishing features, none." In short, the average Frenchman recruited into the managerial ranks is mass-produced and looks like everyone else.

Why the uniformity? First of all, because certain structures inevitably produce a certain type. Second, because the corporate world is basically exclusive, given that everyone who is not "average" is not welcome there. In this way companies reproduce the constipation of the society as a whole: puritan America gets the rigid corporations it deserves. Indeed, the selection methods no longer work, since the number of candidates applying for a position is far greater than the number of people likely to land the post. Companies are submerged with résumés, and since "you can't hire everybody," they might as well reserve the spots for the right people. Especially since the "right" people are always the same.

I'm not trying to wave the sugar-coated banner of some imperialist vision of "United Colors of Benetton" here, but prospective employees really are judged on their age, nationality, and gender, statistics that are irrevocable. Any health problems or career snags are easy to spot on a CV, and count as a strike against you. You say you're handicapped? We recognize your right to work, but not here: try some other firm. You've done some time? It will be mighty hard to find work. Everyone loves *Les Misérables,* but no one would want to hire Jean Valjean, the bighearted ex-con.

The place in the business world for blacks, Arabs, foreigners, and "young people from immigrant backgrounds," as we discreetly call them, is even less enviable. They are very poorly represented in managerial positions. And this is not only because such people are more likely to succeed in sports or the entertainment field. As for homosexuals, while "sensitive men" may enjoy a certain status in professions connected with the creative arts or fashion world, the general consensus is that they have no place in business. Homosexuality simply won't do; that's just the way it is. The result of this ambient homophobia is that with equal competency, a gay has little chance of rising to a directorial post.

In the corporate world, some people are more equal than others, and women are far less equal than most. They earn less than men at the same level and have greater difficulty reaching positions of responsibility. Why is this? Simply because they are less visible after the hours of six or seven p.m. and therefore are seldom available during the strategic hours when the firm closes ranks and counts its diehards. Studies have proven what we all suspected: family life is a handicap to the professional success of women, whereas it constitutes an asset for men. Go figure! Too bad if the mother of small children performs her job better than the rest and is more efficient—which, as I have seen for myself, is often the case. She doesn't write the rules of the game: men do.

It's a well-known fact that men spend more time at work than their female counterparts. This can be explained by their insatiable predatory instincts as well as by their casual approach to banal household chores. In France they take responsibility for a mere 20 percent—which, you must admit, will never wear anyone out. Since women slave away at home more than men, they are twice as likely as men to work part-time, which again feeds the inequalities and makes it all the more impossible to break the glass ceiling separating them from the sources of power. As a result, in the upper echelons of power—that is, among the well-heeled battalions of the executives—only 5 percent are women. Statistics don't always tell the whole story, but these don't leave much out.

Equality in the workplace is therefore a far-off dream. One is tempted to bang one's fist and demand quotas of female corporate executives, but it's not clear that this would help matters any. Luckily there's some consolation in the fact that men have a much shorter life expectancy than women, and that they are four times more likely to commit suicide. It's a terrible inequality, but there has to be some justice in the world.

The Hollow Man(ager)

The manager of yore, who exuded hierarchy and status, is a thing of the past. Being a "manager" doesn't mean much anymore, except to indicate someone who has completed a course of study and whom you can't ask to sweep the floor, at least in big businesses, since this isn't a problem in small companies. "Manager" is a title, not a function. It's better to be one than not. Since you spend all day doing the job of the person above you, the higher up you are, the less you have to do. The more important you are, the less you have to work: it's one of the golden rules of the workaday world. That said, it's better not to be too high up either, since you spend all your time performing, like politicians, who quite shamelessly do nothing but have to do it in public, in plain view. You have to like to do that sort of thing. For my part, if I have nothing to do, I prefer being at home or at the movies.

What does a manager do? He is, of course, a masterly manipulator of jargon, but that's not all: he's also a "team coordinator," "catalyst," "visionary," and—why not?—a "rejuvenator." He is no longer someone with particular qualifications but someone who sets things in motion. He's not looking to build an empire, and he manipulates people as opposed to things. He doesn't address concrete tasks or urgent problems; he's there to give "face time." The authority he enjoys over his team is dependent on the "trust" he inspires in his group, thanks to his "communications skills" and his ability to "listen," which he demonstrates in his one-to-one dealings with others. Youthful, cheerful, sexy, the manager maintains the illusion that he is free to choose, even to create. Freed of the burden of ownership and the constraints of corporate hierarchy, our modern manager believes in nothing. Unlike the Soviet "new man," he espouses no cause and feels not the slightest loyalty to the firm he works for. He has little interest in "a job well done," for, when you come right down to it, his ideal of success is empty. On this point as well as many others, René-Victor Pilhes, author of the novel *The Provocateur,* offers enlightenment: "The business administrator is neither accountant nor technician nor salesman; I think he organizes a bit of everything. . . . [T]he path of administration leads to what is called management. Management consists of stripping, as much as possible, all projects, statistics, organizations, transactions—in short, all imaginable decisions—of their emotional components. This is why, for a big-time manager, there is no difference among religions, political regimes, unions, etc."

Shame on those who think, who want, who spend their whole lives doing the same thing! Pride and the bitter scramble for profit, typical of the old world of merchandise, have no place in the volatile and fluid world demanded by big business. Appearances are more important than the quality of the work done; reputation and the recognition of success count more than real accomplishment. From the heavy to the lightweight, from steel to paper—this sums up the progress of capitalism.

Culture and the Manager: The Marriage of the Carp and the Hare

What does the manager know how to do? Nothing precise, really. He is a "generalist." He has studied at the best schools: an eastern prep school, an Ivy League college, a reputable business school where he didn't learn much besides how to land a job. He reads the editorials of two or three individuals who repeat commonplaces and hackneyed phrases, and peppers his speech with the latest buzzwords. Our man (or woman) never examines anything in depth. Why bother? Getting bogged down in facts or numbers doesn't clarify a thing; it only makes them more complicated. One must therefore avoid such things at all costs. "It's a good thing our companies are not in the hands of intellectuals," exclaims one of characters in Pilhes's *The Provocateur.* "What would happen to our consumer society?"

Let's be clear: the basic manager is uncultured, which is not surprising, given the impoverished nature of the world he comes from. For him, culture is a stratagem for showing off at dinner parties. Let's face it, even he knows that the sleek BMW or the gold bracelet is a bit vulgar, but a well-chosen quote is something else again. Realizing that the veneer of culture can give managerial polish, a certain unexpected depth, businesses have taken to offering costly educational programs to its most promising prospects.

These take the form of courses taught by academics lured into the service of a successful economy, most often in the form of a generous stipend. They are happy to earn more money than they do at the university, waylaying the classics and reducing to simplified summaries the "Western Civ" once reserved for an idle elite. At least that elite actually used to read books and listen to music—you won't believe this!—for *pleasure*. Is it possible?

Our high-flying executives have never had the time to read Michel Foucault, listen to a Mozart opera, see a Fellini film. Never. They are too busy. They'll tell you themselves: they're very, very busy. Busy with what? Well, with their obligations, commitments. And what are they committed to do? Having meetings. And what are the meetings for? Organizing work, theirs and other people's. Is this really more useful than reading Balzac's *La comédie humaine* (*The Human Comedy*), whose works tell you a lot about their own tribe, the nature and limits of their ambitions? One does wonder. . . .

This is why we are managed by *Homo economicus cretinus,* the most highly developed and widespread type of the "new man" engendered by big business.

The Idiots You Rub Shoulders With

Engineers and Salesmen: A Stalemate

Given the vast quantity of paperwork it produces, one might imagine that business would need people who know how to write a sentence containing a subject and a predicate. Curiously enough, this is not the case, and it dislikes those whom it refers to scornfully as "literary types." The latter "don't know how to do a thing" and are "daydreamers." Engineers, on the other hand, know how to get things done. They've studied mathematics—and math, as everyone knows, is the science of rationality.

So the engineer is in touch with reality and tries to get to the heart of things without overcomplicating matters. He is wary of his fellow man—and even more so of women, who are by nature unreliable and a source of endless complication. He dreams of total automation, down to the last nanometer and "in real time," engendered by machines that function in such a way that it's only necessary to push a button to get a result. The engineer is out of sync with the rest of us. He can be funny, but often unintentionally. His eccentricities would make him pleasant company in the cafeteria, if he weren't such an oaf.

He waits for the day when everything will run like a well-oiled machine; he likes to solve problems, and when there aren't any, he creates them. This explains why he is a whirlwind of completely useless activity, for which we thank him. To counterbalance the influence of engineers, the corporation unfortunately hires salesmen, who are often pretentious idiots convinced that everything can be bought and sold.

One can see why there are frequent conflicts between the two groups. When the engineers are at the controls, the salesmen are recruited to promote and make commercial sense of the engineers' latest breakthroughs. But that's not easy! Just remember the Concorde: a technological jewel but a money pit. When the salesmen are at the helm, on the other hand, they talk of nothing but reduction of costs, and make it their business to prune, with great machete strokes, the superfluous but sometimes amusing activities dreamed up by our inventive engineers.

Big business, caught between technology and its

pocketbook, therefore has two legs going in opposite directions—so it's not surprising that it often stumbles!

The Consultant: It's Always Insulting to Be Taken for a Jerk

Nowadays, it's unthinkable to raise a child without an educational consultant to teach him how to read and a tutor to help him assimilate the inanities poured into his ears at school. We live in a world of generalized support. You have to wonder how, without outside help, without therapists or cognitive specialists, humanity ever managed to invent the printing press or build cathedrals (a real mystery, which lends credence to the very serious thesis that the pyramids and other wonders of the ancient world were built by extraterrestrials).

The same goes for big business. Today's organizations are supposed to be "self-educating" and full of "creative" individuals, but they still need help to give birth to new skills and new ideas. A new profession has come into being: the *coach,* whose role is to serve as a personal guide who helps each person develop his or her true potential. Since businesses want to use all the capabilities of a human being, to allow them to actualize their full potential, the coaches keep watch over the seeds and make sure that they sprout. These coaches, in fact, are nothing more than advisers, branded to appear more modern and up-to-date.

And coaches do in fact fill the important social demand for authenticity and freedom. Doesn't "new management" promise that each individual will no longer be a mere instrument but will be able to realize his or her deepest aspirations?* But this so-called freedom is to big business what pornography is to sexual liberation: a poor substitute.

The coach is not the only parasite on the back of the beast. Big business shells out millions annually for a multitude of auditing and advising "specialists," who are paid to say whatever their client wants to hear and

*This ground was already covered in the political activism of the 1960s! Business recycles everything, even themes that, at a given moment, appeared to liberate us from antiquated forms of power and hierarchy.

confirm the decision-makers' powers of intuition. The strategic or organizational visions of the consultant must be presented in the form of austere and often illegible documents including long lists of "bullet points," accompanied by graphs full of symbols and arrows indicating the many interactions intended to make the presentation more coherent. When our consultant has only two ideas—and that's already a lot—he expresses them in the form of a matrix. The message at the heart of this managerial patchwork reads something along the lines of: "When the building works, everything works," "Electricity is essential to lighting," "The market has reached maturity, meaning many consumers have already bought the product," etc. The consultant loves to invent solutions to obvious problems, such as suggesting cutbacks when the results are bad, or recommending diversification to a business that's making money.

Our adviser basically serves no other purpose than to force employees to accept restrictions across the board or to standardize behavior: "Everyone fall in!" is the credo of the consultant as he breaks down opened doors.

The Useless, the Submissive, and the Goof-offs

Business loves to make categories; it finds them reassuring. In business newspeak, there are, first and foremost, the consumers, who fall into different demographics: from "teenagers" to "aging baby boomers," from "singles" to "dinks" (double income, no kids), not to mention "influentials," "bobos" (bourgeois bohemians), and "early adopters." New categories appear every year. If there are categories of buyers, are there also types of workers? Yes: there are "seasoned professionals," "junior managers," "natural salesmen," "high flyers," and "qualified managers."

I find this verbal jumble unconvincing and want to propose two different typologies that can be applied to the business world. The first is mine; the second was suggested by the psychoanalyst Jacques Lacan,*

*See my penultimate best seller, *Lacan sans peine* (*Lacan Made Easy*) (Carignan, Quebec: Alain Stanké, 2002).

who had more to say than just incomprehensible things about the unconscious intended only for professionals.

Maier's typology: there are three categories of people—the sheep, the pests, and the loafers. The sheep are most numerous: they walk slowly, never try to change anything, never question the status quo, and never take the slightest initiative that might have any effect whatsoever. In short, they are weak and inoffensive. As for the pests, they're the ones who wreak havoc in the entire department they work in, pitting people against one another, poisoning the general atmosphere, and causing nervous breakdowns among their colleagues. Luckily, they are rarer than the first group, but they do a lot more damage. The third, the loafers, are not too visible: discreet, they vaguely scorn the sheep and steer as far as possible from the pests; their only aim is to do as little as possible.

Lacan's typology: there are the bastards, the cynics, and the weaklings. The bastard hijacks the place of the Other, bossing people around in the name of what they want. The bastard tries to rule the people around him, to mold them to his vision. He's the boss who exploits you, underpays you, and then tries to convince you that he has your best interests at heart. The cynic, on the other hand, is ruled only by his whims, but he doesn't try to impose these on others (and in any case the others couldn't really care less). He's the one who calls in sick for two weeks every time he gets a cold, and shamelessly makes other people do his work for him under the pretext that he has other fish to fry in life, such as judo, women, poker, you name it. He devotes all his energy to his passion. In the great game of life he's out strictly for himself. Does he win? Yes, you have to admit that he doesn't fare too badly because he knows how to steer clear of the bastards. These two types are very different from the weaklings. Docile, gullible, willing, the weakling (who is not necessarily stupid) allows himself to be ensnared in the rhetoric of the Other, to the point of getting bogged down in it. For he is passive enough to let himself be led by anyone who wants to take charge! In big business, and in fact everywhere, these perfect subordinates are legion: zealous, servile with the powerful and disdainful toward the rest, ready to identify themselves with whatever system they are placed in. No society can function without them, and it is precisely their vast number that makes any real change unlikely.

Now it's up to you to make connections between the two paradigms: "We'll review things in the morning" but "Don't lose any sleep over it."

People You'll Never See

There are certain idiots whom you will never rub shoulders with, and this is for two reasons: one, because they move in high circles you don't have access to; two, because they span the business galaxy like shooting stars before disappearing into black holes that suck them up forever.

First, a bit of history. Never before the 1980s did big business hold such an important position in French society. Up until then, the business world didn't get good press in France. It was considered exploitative and alienating, and the self-made man was perceived as an upstart in a country that put a premium on the distance between social classes. Then everything changed, as the culture of political engagement and grand social projects fell into crisis. Since there's nothing else to do, let's start a company!

The symbol of this upheaval was Bernard Tapie, great preacher of the cult of performance, model of dynamism, and the darling of the media thanks to his utterly showbiz personality. I remember the dismaying television show *Ambition,* aired during prime time, in which a powerful, relaxed, and determined Bernard Tapie strode down the central aisle before climbing to the podium to the rhythm of an old tune that went:

It's never too late to change
Make your own revolution
And come winds or high water
Defend your ambitions.

To think that I was twenty years old at the time! But it gets worse: while everyone gushed over the image of the winner and the corporate boss, the idea of a "right to succeed" crystallized in a decidedly exacting public. After the "right to bear children" for sterile women, the "right to sexuality" for the handicapped, how long before we have the "right to clone" for the madmen of science?

Tapie's dream did not in fact last very long. The myth of free enterprise was already beginning to fade by the end of the 1980s. We note that the myth did not prevent the crash of 1987, did not protect against unemployment. While the competitive mirage of the 1980s implied that anyone could succeed, today's rhetoric, which is much more negative, plays on the fear that any citizen can fall through the cracks. And in fact this is what happened to Bernard Tapie, pariah of the corporate and political worlds after a meteoric career that lasted as long as a rose before smelling as bad as dirty money and bribes.

The saga continued with Jean-Marie Messier, who also ended up tripping over his gigantic wings. He's the coddled narcissist who was once praised to the skies before being pilloried in public. As the expression goes, "The Tarpeian Rock is right next to the Capitoline," meaning that he succeeded brilliantly before crashing in flames. Because of his inflated ego, the smart-asses in the media nicknamed Messier J6M, *"Jean-Marie Messier, moi-même maître du monde,"* which translates as "Jean-Marie Messier, myself master of the world." The guy just loved to be photographed, and in his glory days you could admire his twenty-million-euro house (paid for by his company, Vivendi) and the leather seats of his private jet in magazines everywhere.

We should have known better. This degree-laden individual (l'École Polytechnique, École nationale d'administration) belongs to the arrogant caste of accountants who put in time in the public sector—where, at the higher levels, there isn't much craft to learn, since one basically owns all of France and the French. As head of the company Générale des Eaux (General Company of Waterworks, renamed Vivendi), he could have learned the craft of water and waste management—but why bother? Water is boring and waste is dirty. Using the money of these two not-so-glamorous sectors, he built a media empire from scratch by promoting so-called synergies, which were nothing more than a consultant's wet dream.

The famous "French cultural uniqueness," whose death J6M, prophet of a new era, once proclaimed, is not in fact dead. It's just not what people thought it was. The French cultural uniqueness is not so much the collection of distinctive national characteristics that make France the often absurd and occasionally marvelous place it is, but the consistency with which our fine country allows itself to be dazzled by charlatans.

V.

Extra, Extra: Big Business Is Doomed!

Does big business have lead in its wings? No one believes in it anymore, and it's getting tangled up in its own contradictions. Let's review these contradictions. Just remember that I'm no Marxist.

Flexibility Is Theft

In the name of "flexibility," that sacred rallying cry of executives, "too much" has become the company motto. Since the mid-eighties, the idea that businesses perform too many activities, employ too many people, and are weighed down by too many objectives has taken hold. And so business has decided to change. The trend is to divest a great number of functions and tasks and to subcontract everything that does not belong to the "core business." The typical model of modern business is a compact center surrounded by a nebula of suppliers, subcontractors, freelancers, temporary workers, and sister firms that allow for a variable workforce based on demand. The workers themselves should be organized in small multitasking and decentralized teams, for whom the client is the real boss.

And if its promoters are to be believed, a frenzy of change seems to have taken hold of the corporate world. Countless propaganda campaigns follow one after the other in rapid succession to make sure we all understand the "direction" of the reforms and become "players" in the new game. In the meantime, the company regularly renames its services, reorganizes its workforce, and rearranges its offices. For many, reorganizing is progress, but it's also a way to justify the boss's salary, because what else is a boss paid for?

Well, to give the employees the impression that there's something going on! Everything must change so that everything can remain the same.

This culture of permanent revolution, inspired by corporations such as General Electric and IBM, is to the company what the Chinese Cultural Revolution was to politics: a dream of perpetual change that is nothing more than a chimera. Mao Zedong would not be very surprised. Reshuffle the cards, challenge all assumptions to keep people on their toes, prevent established gains from crystallizing: this is precisely what Mao tried to do in China, sacrificing millions of lives in the process. Fortunately, in the West, where things are done in a more civilized manner (at least since 1945), Mao's disturbing ideal remains just a fantasy.

What nevertheless remains of this surreal goal—that an organization divest itself of the material world of basic necessities—is in the shedding of jobs. This makes it possible to "trim the fat" as well as—why not?—get rid of the factory, which is heavy, ugly, dirty, and graceless. Serge Tchuruk, CEO of the telecommunications group Alcatel, had the inspired idea of jettisoning his own factories: the fewer you have, the fewer employees, the fewer paychecks—and the better paid the CEOs. George Fischer, head of Eastman Kodak, responsible for the greatest number of layoffs in 1997 (20,100 jobs cut), received that same year a portfolio of stock options estimated at $60 million. Even better, Jean-Marie Messier increased his revenues by 66 percent in 2001, earning 5.1 million euros while his company, Vivendi, lost 13 billion. It's like sand in the hourglass: the more the companies lose money, personnel, and factories, the more the bosses gain (financially). Always less on one side, always more on the other. How long can this go on?

As a Chinese proverb might put it (Mao would have appreciated this): "The day the workers eat the bait, the big fish will get a mouthful of water."

Two Modes of Discourse, Zero Brains

Caught between two policies, you die, the victim of your own contradictions. Such is the risk big business takes by wavering between two incompatible modes of discourse: that of obedience and that of freedom.

Extra, Extra: Big Business Is Doomed!

You have to face the facts: a company over a certain size becomes a woolly mammoth. It's a wheezing old woolly mammoth, organized into personal fiefdoms, crushed under the weight of tradition and customs, bound by complex salary grids and hierarchical strata as impenetrable as a jungle.

At the same time—and here lies the paradox—our mammoth wants to be relaxed, laid-back, and cool, so it reorganizes and eliminates positions right and left in order to be more flexible. The claim to "wish their employees well," the absence of autonomy, and obligatory obedience go hand in hand with cynicism, layoffs, and the exploitation of the individual as a simple resource. Paternalism and amorality are the teats of this velvet barbarism. In fact, big business is a living contradiction, trying as it does to reconcile corporate stultification and dexterity of presentation and succeeding only in rendering each meaningless.

The schizophrenic mammoth that we call big business vacillates between two ways of talking, between two defensive postures. The first, which smacks of Stalinist propaganda, is a neocommunist discourse that glorifies a return to an idealized past, with nationalized industries, a nonglobal economy, a blueprint for social welfare based on simpleminded egalitarianism, and powerful, old-fashioned labor unions. The second, which reeks of a pseudo-hip and -energetic conservatism, is a free-market discourse whose brutality is camouflaged by the new communications and information technologies, free trade, versatility, and self-fulfillment. Both are clearly a tissue of unilateral stupidities, but it is always amusing to see other people spouting such idiocy with conviction. By refusing to subscribe to either one, you can at least have the satisfaction of feeling intelligent.

The Spirit of Capitalism: Where Is It?

How do you get employees to work in a lasting and ever-engaged way? "The way things stand today," as my boss says, smacking his lips with a slobber, it's anybody's guess. Still, for big business to attract relatively intelligent people and make productive middle managers out of them, it has to prove that it makes a contribution to society as a whole, and that its goal is not only more wealth for those who already have enough.

If it is to function, it must give people reasons to act, to work, to want to advance in its ranks. At the outset, according to the philosopher Max Weber, capitalism was imbued with the Protestant work ethic. At that time it was buoyed by a rather ascetic "spirit," something like the ghost of a religious belief. And now? Have self-fulfillment and the desire, not only for a job, but for a meaningful job, fallen completely by the wayside?

The answer seems to be yes. Look around: there's nothing to believe in. It's pointless to put your life on the line, for economics or anything else. History is full of superfluous battles in which people have killed one another in order to decide if they should be French or German, Catholic or Protestant. After so many lost battles, it's better to overload our lives with the petty pleasures spewed out by our consumer society: renting a DVD at Blockbuster, buying a customized car with Mickey Mouse on the windshield, or ordering caviar online for home delivery.

If there are no causes for which to get up in the morning, then this means, according to the philosopher Alexandre Kojève, a great admirer of Hegel, that there is no more history. All that's left is for us to consume *more* and *more* in an effort to set ourselves *more* and *more* apart from our neighbors who are purchasing the same brands we believe are so distinctive. We are resembling one another *more* and *more*.

But are the bloodless struggles and small satisfactions of a prosperous and self-satisfied free-market economy enough to satisfy our most excessive tendencies? I have my doubts. In each of us lies a dormant brute, a saint, a madman, or a hero—your choice: pick the figure that most appeals to you and do whatever it takes to be worthy of it. But don't forget that this is incompatible with filling your cart at Whole Foods Market or drinking a beer in front of the TV after work.

Meaninglessness as a Newly Discovered Universal Law

A naïve person might think that big business is looking for one thing and one thing alone: profit. This is often true, of course, but not always—or at least it's not so simple, because profit is paradoxical: everyone talks about it, but no one knows exactly what it is. It arises from the interval between what is sold and what is bought; between the merchandise and the product as it appears on the market. Marx thought that one part of this discrepancy resulted from a theft perpetrated by the capitalist at the expense of the worker. Perhaps if the capitalist economy runs after this elusive gap, it is because pleasure always lies in the space, the pause, between what is offered and what is received, in the difference between what is taken and what is kept. In other words, what keeps all of humanity running is an ever-elusive little bonus!

It's a big mistake to think that reality is rational. Business is not simply a matter of cash flow and results. It is also, and more often than it should be, a universe of the absurd. In business, the ultimate task is to create another task. This is how the business world wastes so much time and resources. The bigger it is, the more it can allow itself to squander, as if this munificence were the proof of its strength and its importance. You can only gaze in awe at the riot of completely useless paperwork it produces:

project descriptions, minutes of meetings and conferences, business and department plans, mission statements . . . What a prolific output!

This profusion inevitably leads to duplications. There are people and even teams doing the same thing, simultaneously but independently developing the same product. Sometimes this even happens in triplicate and—let's not mince words!—even in quadruplicate. The more employees needlessly repeating the work of others, the more convinced they are of the importance of what they are doing.

No fat trimming could ever do away with such excess. It is to business what love, celebration, and art are to life: necessary outlets for surplus energy and strength. One might even imagine that business practices its own version of what Marcel Mauss calls a potlatch, which, among Native Americans of the Northwest, consists of amassing great surpluses and riches in order to be able to squander them. As Scott Adams writes in *The Dilbert Principle,* "Nothing defines humans better than their willingness to do irrational things in the pursuit of phenomenally unlikely payoffs. This is the principle behind lotteries, dating, and religion." And so the firm, so prodigious in useless expenditures, tries at the same time to reorganize itself to be more efficient. Perhaps it feels guilty! I can understand that. With each new year I decide to go on a strict diet after my holiday excesses, then abandon my boring diet a few days later with a binge of wining and dining, only to cut down again with the coming of spring. . . . This slightly chaotic stop-and-start may not be the best way to move forward, but it is certainly the most human.

The New Economy: The Latest Flash in the Pan

For a few years (three years at most) before bowing out in 2001, the new economy was capitalism's latest toy. It embodied the dream of a business that makes nothing, costs as little as possible, and limits itself to buying and selling. In short, business *lite,* which "creates value" almost by miracle, since it produces as little as possible and avoids getting its hands dirty. The model was Enron, the "new-style" American energy company, which decided to divest all of its power plants in order to devote its energies to the oldest profession in the world: that of the middleman, the "trader." The dot-com formula was on the rise, attached at the end of any old word, transforming the Old World into the New. How about this: somethingfornothing.com. It was not so much dot-com as dot-con.

At the beginning of the twenty-first century, you needed only to go out to dinner to run across an ambitious young man who had just quit his job in order to create or join a promising new start-up. And the rest of us, the dinosaurs from the "old economy," frozen in a salary grid and snoozy career, felt very, very old. These newfangled businesses exuded *cool:* between the go-karting weekends, the video game consoles, and foosball matches, young adults strolled about with skateboards tucked under their arms and discussed their rave experiences around the watercooler.

But in 2002 Enron went bankrupt, followed shortly thereafter by WorldCom, while Jean-Marie Messier, the new economy messiah, was joined by Ron Sommer (Deutsche Telekom) and Robert Pittman (AOL Time Warner) in being forced to resign. They all sold fantasies before tripping over their Superman costumes. The result: a disturbing domino effect.

Extra, Extra: Big Business Is Doomed!

When Enron and WorldCom collapsed, victims of the two largest bankruptcies in history, America itself stumbled. Things are a bit different in France: when Vivendi, France Telecom, and Alcatel caught cold, the state coughed, and the taxpayers ended up footing the bill. The return of stability, but at great cost. If you want security, you have to pay for it.

During this period, the multitude of start-ups created by young people convinced they were reinventing the wheel were swept away like wisps of straw. The whippersnappers got whippersnapped. Was the economic system itself jeopardized? *No, no, it will recover! It always has in the past, even though on occasion some rather unpleasant things have happened as the machine sputtered back to life. All we need is a good war, a spending spree in khaki, the kind of event that usually boosts the economy. When you keep on destroying, there obviously comes a moment when you have to rebuild. The Bush administration understands this. Why deprive ourselves?*

And now for a moral moment. Why was the new economy a con game? Because you can't turn your back with impunity on the reality principle that a business without clients or annual turnover is forced to slide the key under the door. The crash in the technologies of the future (Internet, telecom) demonstrates that the corporate world is chasing a dream: the dream of easy money, the lure of gain with no pain. Psychoanalysis would say that the corporate world is trying to escape the law of castration; Marxism would say that big capital is trying to wave away the underlying tendency for the rate of profit to decrease.

And I say: New economy, when will you come back? Unlike other spectators, I heartily applaud when the lazy earn more than the hardworking, when the bad guy triumphs, when the black sheep marries the beautiful saloon girl, Peggy, and all to the tune of a song by Ennio Morricone. *Wake up, Corinne,* says the voice of reason, *you aren't in a Western; this is real life.* Maybe that's what's really wrong with the economy; maybe it doesn't dream enough!

Globalization: The Worm in the Apple

The world itself is the new horizon. René-Victor Pilhes prophesied this already a few decades ago in

Extra, Extra: Big Business Is Doomed!

The Provocateur: "That was a time when the rich countries, bristling with industry, stuffed with stores, discovered a new faith, a project worthy of the efforts made by man for millennia: to make the world into one enormous corporation." Under this relentless barrage of the wisdom of nations, we're struck dumb. Whoever doesn't understand the New World Order is useless, obsolete: global individuals, global businesses, global nations. The world as a single mine of raw materials, a single breeding ground for labor, the world as common market, as vast terrain for the board game of finance. The world unified beneath the banner of a single dream, a dream of oneness, sameness. Everywhere the same brands, the same products, the same people. The twenty-first century will be international or not at all—such is the rallying cry of the neoliberals—and no great revolution is required. Or is it a new way to imagine the Armageddon? How does the world end? Not with a bang but with a Starbucks.

And, of course, this is all necessary, very, very necessary. Will the end of history take the inevitable form of free enterprise, spreading its tentacles farther and farther, across seas, across borders? This has already been imagined; the German philosopher Hegel thought that the evolution of human societies would not be infinite but would come to an end the day humanity perfected a form of society that satisfied its deepest, most fundamental needs. The problem is that in the twentieth century, everything that was presented as inevitable turned out to be, in fact, totalitarian. We must beware: after the law of history that so-called communism obeyed and the law of nature that supposedly governed Nazism, do we now have a law of profit that governs capitalism?

Luckily, voices are being raised in protest. More and more of globalization's cheerleaders are defecting from the ranks. Some of the more committed supporters of global capitalism have noisily changed camps over the last few years. There are some big fish among them: no less than the speculator George Soros, who owes his colossal fortune to the interdependence of the financial markets, and the Nobel Prize–winning economist Joseph Stiglitz, ex–vice president of the World Bank.* (Small parenthesis: God only knows why public opinion and the media are always most in-

*See George Soros, *George Soros on Globalization* (New York: PublicAffairs, 2002) and Joseph Stiglitz, *Globalization and Its Discontents* (New York: W. W. Norton, 2003).

terested in people who bite the hand that feeds them. By this logic, will *Bonjour Laziness,* which thumbs its nose at big business, be a hit? We'll see. . . .) Standing up against globalization has become trendy! If it inspires mistrust among the very people who were its most devoted advocates, then the worm is definitely in the apple. Let us nurture it, so that the little worm will one day be big.

VI.

Why There's No Risk in Disengaging Yourself

If you have nothing to gain by working hard, you don't have much to lose in doing nothing. You can subvert your company through your own passivity, and without running any risks. It would be a shame not to take advantage of this opportunity. Professions, authority, work itself, are on the way out. It's a chance not to be missed. But pretending to be busy isn't always that easy. . . .

Work: No More Professions

Professions are a thing of the past, and many managers don't really know what they're paid for. Whole spheres of activity as well as many positions (consultants, experts, managers) serve no purpose whatsoever, except as excuses for "managing" paperwork, flourishing your Magic Marker in front of the whiteboard, or hotdogging in meetings. Utterly superfluous tasks abound, such as developing a "policy" on the drafting of protocols, participating in a work group on the development of a suggestion system for product improvement, and taking part in a seminar on the subject "We Foresee the Need for Internationally Integrated Solutions on a Global Scale." Not to mention devising new forms for questionnaires, concocting new procedures, drafting memos more than two pages long (no one will read them), and, even simpler, inventing "pilot" projects, most of which will fail or end up having nothing to do with the initial idea.

What's more, the utterly opaque titles given to

these positions serve as clever smoke screens. Just what is a "partnering consultant," a "quality maintenance representative," or an "assignment normalizer"? Try simply saying "I work in business" at the next dinner party you're invited to, and you'll see that no one, absolutely no one, asks you "Doing what?" or even "What firm?"—except out of pity.

Even secretaries don't have real jobs anymore—that is, if you can still find a secretary, since they are a dying breed. The typist of the sixties, with eyeglasses and a miniskirt, sitting behind her typewriter, at the boss's beck and call, is but a distant memory. In "trimming away" these jobs, the opportunities for adultery have been sacrificed to a more restrained bureaucratic puritanism in which the only pleasures are those of the mouse pad and monitor. The secretaries who have survived the move to computerized offices have diplomas and do the same work as you: they sort, classify, and produce paper.

To think that they are at your service would not be so much a mistake as an unforgivable offense. You'd better be very pleasant to secretaries, because they suffer from huge inferiority complexes, due to the unjustified disdain with which society regards so-called menial tasks. There is little prestige in being directly in the service of someone else, and the sense of degradation associated with such positions is such that those who hold them are not likely to be considerate or efficient with clients, for fear of being seen as flunkies. The problem is that we are all, to greater and lesser degrees, in the service of someone. To be of service without being servile—that's the name of the game, the "challenge."

Yet, although the typist has disappeared, her work has not: now you do it yourself. Keeping track of vacation time, following up on invoicing, chasing down clients, making hotel and airplane reservations, little maintenance tasks, the mail. Hello, chores. There are so many chores like these that they become ends in themselves. It is now obvious that doing away with positions simply displaces the work onto others. You're turned into a "two-in-one" manager, when it's not "three-in-one." Since most companies have reduced the managerial ranks, there are fewer and fewer bosses, so you become a manager, his boss, and his secretary all rolled into one. Holy trinity of the corporate world, hear the prayers of us paper-swamped managers!

But in reality you have never been so free as you are in this morass of paperwork, precisely because of the vague and imprecise nature of the tasks assigned you. No one knows exactly what you're doing, and if they ask, don't under any circumstance say that you're busy re-sorting all the paper in front of you into different piles.

No More Authority: Take Advantage of It

"There's nobody in charge here, it's every man for himself, there's no one at the top, there's no more respect, this is going to come to a bad end, we need a real leader!" So say those who miss the good old days. Families aren't the only place where there's no more authority; it's gone out of fashion everywhere. Psychoanalysts—teachers, too—are worried about this dehiscence (yes, I like rare words, words that my bosses don't understand): they're beginning to tear their hair out.

As for me, I'm rubbing my hands in glee: it's a golden opportunity. If you are a manager, no one will give you any direct orders; no one will ever tell you that you are stupid or incompetent. The corporate world is permissive, and conviviality is a must. But be careful, it's no less oppressive for all that: consensus rules, and it is sacrosanct. The important thing is to respect the rules, the rituals, the status quo. The smooth running of the business is now more important than actually doing business, and the means have become the ends.

How does this play out on a day-to-day basis? The boss expresses a lame opinion; everyone vaguely assents or discusses secondary issues. Those who disagree think about what they're going to eat for dinner, and everyone ends up agreeing. The desire not to disrupt group cohesion is fundamental. The corporate world is ultra soft-core, not a place where you call a spade a spade. Moreover, acquiescence is the sine qua non for rising to the top. Unanimity is crystallized in the business meeting. Meetings, meetings, and more meetings! But is communing with the group spirit and sacrificing yourself to collective rationality (which often is not rational) really work? Let's not have any illusions here: it's a real burden, because getting along with others is by definition difficult, but it's not work. There's a subtle difference.

The company's supreme objective is to encourage the employee to impose on himself things that, under normal circumstances, would be imposed on him from without. This new kind of pressure was first imagined by the British visionary Jeremy Bentham (1748–1832), inventor of the Panopticon system. This was a kind of prison designed so that a single person, hidden in a sort of central office, could oversee hundreds if not thousands of people at once. No one knows exactly whether he is being watched at any given moment, since the guard may have gone off to the john. According to the philosopher Michel Foucault, the Panopticon is the model of power today, in business and elsewhere: ungraspable, but with tentacles that reach everywhere.

Since authority no longer exists—since it is dispersed in a system that is both omnipresent and impersonal—there can be no real debate, either. People who don't agree with the single party line imposed by their boss often say: "But I won't tell him that." And since no one can tell him, nobody ever says anything, or else they speak so evasively that the words lose their edge and the questioning its point. Everyone fall in line! Eyes front! Mouth shut!

No More Work: A Godsend

So who works in business? Let's not kid ourselves: not that many people. The following story illustrates this. A few large French companies got together to set up intercompany rowing competitions (four oarsmen plus a helmsman). The teams were made up of workers from each of the companies. The directors of one of the companies noticed that for a few years their team always came in last. Cause for upset and investigation: an expert was brought in to analyze what was going on. The expert investigated over a few weeks and in the end concluded that there were four coxswains in the boat and only one rower. The directors were perplexed, and asked the advice of a consultant. The long and the short of his conclusion? We must motivate that rower! (Any similarity to actual companies is of course purely coincidental.) Indeed, a company is often like the Mexican army, in which everyone wants to be the boss, "project head," or "team manager," but no one wants to carry out orders.

France is a country where nobody works. It's a little-known aspect of the "French uniqueness" that the total amount of work done within her borders is unbelievably low in proportion to her population. No need for statistics to understand this; it's enough to hang around the left bank of Paris to understand. There are people all over the place, and you see many adults strolling about, adults of working age who might otherwise contribute to their country's economic strength. But that's the point: their country does not need them. Productivity in France is one of the highest in the world. Consequently, people work for barely thirty years, unemployment rates remain high, and the sacrosanct midweek holidays create the opportunity for very long weekends. As for the thirty-five-hour week that reduced the maximum number of hours with no cut in pay, it whittles away the workweek in favor of ever more demanding leisure activities.

But then, why are managers forever lamenting their lack of time? Indeed, they claim to be working more and more, to be perpetually "running late." There is some truth in this, certainly for subcontractors who work in tight shifts and are subject to strict quality controls. It's also true for the scatterbrains who have accepted "on-site" assignments—sometimes even "near the client"—and who have to grapple with deadlines, squeezed between the market and the organization. But, between us, you have to be a masochist to work under such conditions. So it's normal that the people who accept them risk *karōshi,* the brutal death that strikes down managers in the prime of life (but only in Japan), or the less serious burnout, a common affliction among wage earners in English-speaking countries.

It's a fact that, in France, work is divided in such an unequal manner that, except for a handful of individuals who slave away, the majority have an easy time of it. The managers with degrees from good or average schools who have succeeded in taking cover in the nooks and crannies of a big corporation are lying when they say they're overworked. Some of them, the clever ones, skillfully couch things in vague terms. Thus Jean-Cyril Spinetta, CEO of Air France, with an honesty that does him credit, declared in a recent interview, "I set aside for myself certain periods of time for unwinding."* Translation: he doesn't do a goddamn thing, and he thinks that's all right. Work is dead: long live work!

The Art of Doing Nothing

Since managers give nothing to their companies but their time, their availability, they are laying it on a bit thick when they claim to be overworked. It's their way of saying that they're making sacrifices. Unlike in Germany, where a worker who leaves work late is considered inefficient, in France, as in many other countries, to stay until eight or even nine o'clock when you're "working against the clock" is considered good. This shows that you like your job. In some big companies, people even stay at work overtime to make personal telephone calls, surf the Internet, make free photocopies, read the paper. At least you're not working while you're doing this.

Enjeux - Les Echos, no. 189 (March 2003).

But doing nothing isn't so easy. You have to know how to pretend. Here is some pertinent advice given by the indispensable Scott Adams in his priceless manual, *The Dilbert Principle:* "Never walk down the hall without a document in your hands. People with documents in their hands look as if they're hardworking employees headed for important meetings. People with nothing in their hands look like they're heading for the cafeteria. People with a newspaper in their hands look like they're heading to the bathroom. Above all, make sure you carry loads of stuff home with you at night, thus generating the false impression that you work longer hours than you do." Now you know what you need to know to do nothing.

You can also spend your days in meetings gathering information and putting it back into circulation, but you must be careful not to add anything of value, since that's work. A study recently conducted in the United States lists the average number of e-mails received by a middle manager at eighty-five a day. And you can be sure most of them are completely useless. But this avalanche of messages does have three advantages: it allows for the creation of Internet management positions and keeps those who send them, as well as those who receive them, busy.

For the most ambitious among you, it's first and foremost imperative to be available when the boss walks down the corridor. That is the obsession of Adrien Deume in Albert Cohen's classic novel *Belle du seigneur.* The petty functionary dreams of one thing alone: licking his superiors' boots to work his way up, by hook or by crook, to grade A. Meanwhile, it goes without saying, his wife, the beautiful Ariane, is blissfully cheating on him with his boss, proof that in novels and organizations alike, justice sometimes prevails.

Conclusion

Begin Your Sabotage Tomorrow

The case has been heard and the jury has spoken, and the galleys have emptied. You will never be the "new man" the business world wants you to be: loyal and faithful representative selflessly devoted to the common cause, the boss's creature, zealous servant, worthy scion, suboordinate to the needs of the group. The corporation's claim to mobilizing your whole being to its own advantage leads to the opposite: it makes clear your oppression, to which you should respond, without retreat, irrevocably, by becoming a parasite—subtly but without compromise.

Become instead the firm's detritus, its castoff, a permanent misfit, impervious to manipulation. Become the grain of sand in the machine, the anomaly that defies homogenization. In this way you will escape the implacable law of usefulness and the ever-present myth of the common good, which never made any individual happy.

White-collar dissidents, disengage!

The Ten Commandments Imposed on the Middle Manager

Let's recapitulate. The following is a list of what the firm expects from its employees; its demands are great and often contradictory. The best way to satisfy these demands is not to think about them—a weighty responsiblity. Remember, you're just a number, a small cog in a big machine.

- Work is a gift, your job a privilege. You have a job? Take advantage of your good fortune: many aren't so lucky.

- Don't keep count of your hours. This is the condition for getting a steady job and keeping it.

- Your company expects a lot from you but owes you nothing in return. That's the way it is; call it "market forces" or "economic justice." You have no choice, since there's no future, no social life, no self-fulfillment, no life outside work.

- Obey the rules. In business, everyone has an equal chance, so only the best succeed. The existing rules were put into place by the people on top, who are the most competent. As for you, if you don't succeed, it's not because the dice are loaded but because you don't deserve to succeed. If you fail, you have no one to blame but yourself.

- Be docile and compliant. Consensus is paramount. It's better to be wrong as a group than right on your own. It is better to move forward as a group, never mind in what direction or by what means. Whoever dares to utter a dissenting opinion will be guilty of standing against the common interest.

- Don't think too much about what you're doing. It's pointless, even counterproductive. People who take seriously the tasks assigned to them prevent things from operating smoothly; they're the fanatics who endanger the system.

- Accept without question the way of the corporate world. The managers you rub elbows with at work are mostly white, of native stock, middle-class, heterosexual, and, in the executive suites, male. This should come as no surprise, since foreigners have fewer degrees and qualifications, gays have more problems getting along with others than the rest, women have less time to devote to their jobs than men, etc. Repeat after me . . .

- Get used to repeating, with conviction, the following mantras: the globalization of business is *necessary;* businesses require *compliance;* unemployment among the unqualified is *justifiable;* social security is *too great a burden for society.* When you're finished, start again until you believe what you're saying.

- Learn the managerial credo: the future belongs to pared-down businesses working in networks of many participants, organized into teams or by project, and oriented toward customer satisfaction. In an "uncertain," "complex" environment, this is the only way to "go with the flow." If you don't believe this, don't bother showing up for work tomorrow.

- Use the following words sparingly: "structure," "function," "career," "supervision," "plans," "goals," "hierarchy," "status." These words are passé. Of course, if you work for a big company, all that stuff still exists and has been integrated into the new management credo, which makes things pretty complicated. But it's up to you to figure shit out. Whatever works for you, pal. What do you think you're getting paid for?

In order to shatter the tablets of these ten corporate commandments, I propose these alternatives. And I promise not to talk down to you.

My Ten Counterproposals

- The wage earner is the modern-day slave. Remember that work is not a place for self-fulfillment. If it were, you would know it. You work for your check at the end of each pay period, "full stop," as they say in the corporate world.

- It's useless to try to change the system, or oppose it, since this only reinforces it; challenge makes its existence all the more entrenched. Of course, you can indulge in anarchist jokes, such as setting up a special "call-in-sick day" or adopting the slogan "Steal from your job since your job steals from you." That's always fun, but rebellion was the gambit of the sixties protesters, and we know what became of them: they're your bosses now.

- What you do is ultimately pointless. You could be replaced any day of the week with the first moron who walks in the door. So work as little as possible, and spend a little time (not too much, though) "selling yourself" and "networking" so that you will have backup and will be untouchable (and untouched) the next time the company is restructured.

- You will not be judged on the way you do your work but by your ability to conform. The more buzzwords you mouth, the more colleagues will believe that you are on their side.

- Never, under any circumstances, accept a position of responsibility. You will be forced to work harder with no other benefits than a few extra bucks—"peanuts," as they say, if that.

- In the biggest companies, seek out the most useless positions: those in consultancy, appraisal, research, and study. The more useless your position, the less possible it will be to assess your "contribution to the firm's assets." Avoid operational ("on-site") positions like the plague. The goal is to aim for something "on the sideline": the kind of unproductive "interdepartmental" positions that are of no consequence whatsoever and are subject to no corporate pressure. In short, keep out of sight.

- Once you're safely out of sight, avoid all change. Only the most visible managers are the ones who are let go.

- Learn by discreet signs (clothing quirks, offbeat jokes, warm smiles) to identify people who, like you, doubt the system and have realized just how absurd it is.

- When you're "recruiting" people in temporary positions for the firm (short-term contracts, freelancers, etc.), treat them well: remember, they're the only ones who actually do any work.

- Remind yourself that the ridiculous ideology voiced and promoted by business is not more "true" than the dialectical materialism held up as dogma under the communist system. This, too, will run its course and surely crumble one day. As Stalin himself once said, in the end, death always wins. The trick is knowing when. . . .